The Curious Case of a Man United F.C.'s Fan loyalty's looks can be deceiving

Marcilio Silva, PhD

The Author

Marcilio Angelo e Silva

PhD in Cognitive Psychology (UFPE/BR)
Mphil Cognitive Psychology (UFPE/BR)
Msc in Marketing Management (UCLan/UK)
MA in Sport Management (UCLan/UK)
Full Licentiate in Physical Education (ESEF-UPE/BR)
Acupuncture Training (TAOS Instituto/BR)
Reiki Training (Instituto Guida/BR)
Chiropractic Seitai Training (UNATE/BR)
Bach Floral Training (Centro Logos/BR)
Massotherapy Training (SENAC/BR)

Best Marketing Masters' Student Award
(by CIM – Chartered Institute of Marketing)

Preface

This book is derived from a research done in the Northeast region of England. The main goal was to investigate why football fans are so loyal to the teams they support. More specifically, in the present case study, a very peculiar Man United F.C.'s fan was interviewed in order to understand his reasons to be very much loyal to his team for more than 47 years, since the preferred sport modality followed and watched by his father, for example, was Rugby and not Football.

More than a research, the case study here shown is a very exciting example of the little explored domain of sports fans. It brings up quite surprising information and reveals specific aspects related to the theme of loyalty. From the marketing perspective, it is a modest but solid contribution to a better understanding of how to develop more precise marketing approaches to this specific customers' segment and how to be more understanding about sports fans' needs.

Hopefully you will also have fun reading it all. Maybe not as much as when you attend a Football match, but certainly very close to it!

Marcilio Silva

Contents

Introduction

The influence of global changes in people's lifestyle, behaviour and beliefs is important to be considered in order to obtain a wider view about the changes occurred in sports field in the last decades. The transition from a modernist to a post-modernist era brought with itself a sense of chaos; relativity became for many a philosophy of life; consumerism and materialism emerged as a way of self-affirmation and projection within society (Jameson, 1995; Smart, 1993). As Cova & Sevenfold (1993) cited by Morrison et al. (1999: pp.173) states:

"...The aestheticization of everyday life and consumption are possibly the strongest characteristics of the post-modern European societies. The post-modern human-being is free to pursue choices which can turn each day

into a work of art, resulting in general stylistic promiscuity and playful mixing of codes".

Parallel to the above social phenomenon and not dissociated from it, a commercialization of sport took place in the last decades. This development of the professionalism and commerce in sport has been pointed out as being much more significant from the 1950s because of the event of TV Broadcasting (Mason, 1999). In countries like the USA the amount of money generated by sport events/activities overcome other industries, and reaches the sums of billions of dollars. A good example of it, is the Atlanta Summer Olympics' sponsorship support given by Coca-Cola, Anheuser-Busch, McDonald's, AT&T, VISA, IBM, Kodak, Xerox and some others reaching the total number of eighteen companies which together paid over $500million to have the right to advertise during the games, broadcasts and so forth (Schaaf, 1995). Sports has become a product and a huge way of making profit in all its sense and it is used not anymore with the purpose of offering the general public an entertainment, although sports fans were and are the main reason for the existence of this social phenomenon (Ben-Porat, 2000; Mason, 1999) .

Evidently, Football did not stay out of the commercialization process and to illustrate this, the Joao Havelange's (the former FIFA president) declaration cited by Tapp & Clowes (2000) seems to be more than enough (the estimate football's annual turnover was, at that point in time, of $250bn). To further highlight how Football has become a profitable business in today's society, the following example is used which is cited by Ferrand & Pages (1999) in their article about image management in sport:

> *"Manchester United, for example, in its latest year, to July 1997, received revenue from merchandising which was almost as great as that from gate receipts (£28million compared with £30million)."*

In the last 2 decades players' transactions and salaries were substantially increased and a good example of it was the Brazilian Ronaldo's transference to Inter Milan F.C. for US$ 32million with a contract offering a salary of US$ 500.000 a month. All this without mentioning the other ads contracts signed by the player with Parmalat, Nike, Pirelli and Brahma Beer which together reached the overwhelming salary sum of approx. US$ 3million a month - not mentioning the benefits Inter Milan gained with the exploitation of Ronaldo's image (the author worked for Inter Milan F.C. from 1997 to 2000).

Advertisements were improved in quality and number in stadiums, teams' multi-sponsorship became a practice, broadcasters started to pay huge amount of money for exclusivity, as in the case of BSkyB that paid a staggering £1.024billion at the FAPL's auction to retain its exclusive broadcasting rights for consecutive fourth time (Harbord & Szymanski, 2004). Based upon this, it is plausible to affirm that Football is undoubtedly a business as any other, however at the same time not quite, when it comes to the loyal football supporters' domain.

Because of this continuingly improved trend within sports field, research initiatives have been taking place. For instance, Mason (1999) pinpoints the importance of a better comprehension of the actual sports' products in order for marketers to understand and develop more effective and 'personalized' strategies to suffice the whims of the different consumers of sports' products; this author suggests that from the market of leagues' product four different consumers derive and they are: sports' fans, communities and their sports facilities, television and other media, and corporate ownership (sponsors).

Some authors (e.g. Cova & Cova, 2002) affirm that a 'narcissist' process took place in the present post-modern society, which in a way has been influenced by the development of hi-tech goods. Ben-Porat (2000) suggests that because of such social influences sports' fans can adopt similar attitudes, however, there are other scientific indications (Gwinner

& Swanson, 2003; Bristow & Sebastian, 2001; Manson, 1999; Hunt et al, 1999) that point to the belief that in the case of some types of sports' fans the feeling of attachment, loyalty and self-identification towards a specific social group (a team, athlete, etc.) is still imperative and has been hardly influenced by the postmodernist mentality, and this idea is bolstered by the present research. Inasmuch as what has been said so far, it becomes clear the need for even more new research initiatives, especially in the little explored fans' terrain, as Tapp & Clowes (2000) highlight that only four percent of research in sport has focused on spectators. Shannon (1999) in his article about academic marketing publication, points out that between Sep.1992 and Mar.1999 only 15 articles about spectators, participants and fans have been published in the Sport Marketing Quarterly in the US, for instance; he believes that research in sports marketing should be encouraged. Considering the information above, it is possible to affirm that an even smaller number of researches have been directed at loyal football fan's domain.

This study is very much based upon the belief that loyal football fans are not ordinary consumers, as elements (other than commercial benefits) greatly influence their attitudes and behaviour and this idea is bolstered by Tapp & Clowes (2000). These authors pinpoint that there is an emphasis in the literature that sports' spectators are unique, as consumers and they should be therefore treated differently from those of the "mainstream" commerce. This idea is here supported and believed to be applicable to football as well.

The perspective used in this research is inspired by the social identity theory (Asforth & Mael, 1989) which lends it the premise for the belief that it is because of fans' self-identification that a feeling of attachment towards their supported team emerges and consequently an emotional bound is established. This determines variations in attitudes and behaviour that are not easily passive of explanation (specially from a business perspective) - as in the case of loyal supporters who maintain their loyalty to their teams even if the latter have not been successful for a long time (Bristow & Sebastian, 2001; Hunt et al, 1999). To date, the approach adopted by marketing researchers to address sports fans' issues has been very much positivist with the intention to either classify and typify fans or to explain fans' attitudes and behaviour based mostly on psychographic, (geo)demographic and economic perspectives (Tapp & Clowes, 2000; Mullin et al., 2000). The intention here is not to be cynical about such scientific contributions, as their value on the creation of new knowledge is incontestable. However, because of the current author's personal beliefs, a different approach for this research seems to be more adequate for the study of social phenomena such as football fan's loyalty.

Therefore, the current study proposes a qualitative approach to deeply understand the real reasons why devoted fans (Hunt et al, 1999) are highly loyal to their teams, why and how they become and remain loyal to a team even if it goes through a hardship moment (Bristow & Sebastian, 2001); and how they conceive their relationship with their supported clubs. By finding out such motives, it would possible to understand why the zone of tolerance of devoted Football fans is high (the concept of tolerance zone has been well emphasized in management literature (Lovelock & Wright, 2002; Groenroos, 2000) and it is inextricably related to the assumption that a consistent service delivery is not possible to be achieved because of the heterogeneity of the people involved in the service process. In a nutshell, zone of tolerance is the level of tolerance a consumer has towards a service provided by a company and it will directly be determined by the consumer's conception of quality and emotional attachment to the service provider); also, what is determinant for a loyal football fan's emotional attachment and level of loyalty to their team; and if there exist any relationship between zone of tolerance and loyalty levels. Finally, to understand whether their loyalty is passive of the postmodernism's influence. In addition, based upon such findings it might be possible to improve or even develop marketing strategies to exploit such elements related to football fans' justifications for their loyalty in order to encourage them to become even more loyal to their teams and possibly, to engage in a word of mouth process to convince other less loyal fans of the benefits of becoming a devoted fan. Moreover, such findings would help marketers to promote the emergence of new-devoted fans.

For this study five main assumptions were made. The first one, that devoted football fans do not see themselves as ordinary consumers but as 'indirect owners' and therefore their zone of tolerance (Lovelock & Wright, 2002; Groeroos, 2000) towards their team is high. The second was that the loyalty of devoted football fans to their teams starts from childhood because of family/peer influences. Third, devoted football fans have an emotional attachment to their teams, which is based on regional/community/social status or pride reasons. Fourth, that tolerance and loyalty levels are reciprocally influential and determine the attitude of devoted football fans towards the teams supported by them. Finally, the consumerist and materialistic mentality of postmodernist society does not influence the loyalty of devoted football fans.

As it has already been said, this research kept its focus on football fans only, given the importance football has in British society and internationally as well. Given the fact that there exist different kinds of fans, this research took the case study of a male fan classified as "die-hard" fan (Bristow & Sebastian, 2001) or "devoted" fan (Hunt et al, 1999) that lives in Leyland - Lancashire and supports Man United F.C. It is important to emphasize that the research here proposed did not aim at offering representative findings, but at offering a deep analysis based on the information gathered from the personal perspective of the subject here studied. The intention here is to provide the scientific community with a short and humble but deep contribution to new knowledge about the inner reasons and motivations of devoted football fans associated with the current marketing theories.

Finally, but not least important, ethical issues were carefully addressed in order to preserve the real nature and intention of the research done and to protect the privacy of its participant.

Management & Marketing "x" Football

It is already well known in management literature that services are different from goods-related industry, and yet they possess some characteristics in common. Nonetheless, the managerial approach of each of them must be different (Schmenner, 1986; Shostack, 1987; Lovelock, 1992; Davidoff, 1994; Palmer, 1998; Hoffman & Bateson, 2002). When it comes to identify which classification football clubs fall into it becomes to a certain extent quite difficult, however it could be said that it tends to be more a service provider than a goods-related business.

There are different ways of understanding the nature of services. Norman (2000) highlights some of the differences of services in comparison to goods-related industries such as the intangibility of services, the non-transferability of product ownership, the non-existence of product before the purchasing process, the coincidence of production and consumption, the involvement of customers in the production process and the non-re-sellable characteristic of services' products. Some of the traits previously cited are also found on Lovelock's (1992) description about the nature of services product, which are: the intangibility of the product - people cannot touch but only experience it; the involvement of customers in the provision of a service - characterizing the variability of services product; and its perishability - as an inventory of it cannot be made. The process in service firms is also different from goods-related businesses and according to Schmenner (1986) it can be classified through three basic elements, which are: the 'labour intensity' that basically regards to a ratio amongst physical and human structure; the 'consumer interaction' that is related to the intensity of interaction between customers and a company's stuff; and the 'service customization' that is concerned about how high or low customized the service product is.

Within the services management literature the concept of tolerance zone has also been well emphasized (Lovelock & Wright, 2002; Groenroos,

2000) and it is inextricably related to the assumption that a consistent service delivery is not possible to be achieved because of the heterogeneity of the people involved in the service process. In a nutshell, zone of tolerance is the level of tolerance a consumer has towards a service provided by a company and it will directly be determined by the consumer's perception of quality and emotional attachment to the service provider. A service that is delivered below the level expected by a customer might well frustrate and disappoint them, or otherwise, it will delight them. Consequently, the width of such zone will be directly determined by the extent to which customers will accept quality variations in the service provided, and the level of emotional attachment to the brand in turn will influence their tolerance level. As emotional attachment is necessary for the establishment of loyal attitude, it can be said that the greater the emotional attachment, the wider will be customers' zone of tolerance and level of loyalty to a specific brand. However, Bristow & Sebastian (2001) highlights that non-fan customers' loyalty seems to be a rare phenomenon nowadays. Nonetheless, in the case of sports' fans (here football fans) loyalty does exist and one of the intentions of the present academic work is to understand what triggers this phenomenon.

Taking into consideration what has been previously said about zone of tolerance and loyalty of sports fans and about the trait differences of goods-related and services businesses, it is possible to draw some arguments about football clubs and fans: football clubs can be considered as a combination between a service provider and a goods-related business - football clubs are a service provider because they offer the opportunity for persons (known as fans or spectators) to buy an experience which is the football match itself and all psychological elements related to it, and which has the traits of a service product such as intangibility, inseparability, variability, perishability. They are also goods-related businesses, as they also sell other tangible products such as T-Shirts, balls, caps, magazines and many other souvenirs. Therefore, the marketing approach to be used in this sector theoretically would include tools and techniques applicable for both industries in order to achieve the best results; however, this assumption is arguable as the goods-related side of such organizations is deeply influenced by their services-side. Furthermore, when it comes to determine what motivates a loyal football fan have to consume products from their supported team, it becomes a quite difficult task, as other elements such as fans' loyalty feelings and self-identification can play a very important role on the determination of such unique customers' attitude. Moreover, it is difficult to comprehend whether the traditional marketing principles and strategies to be used by football clubs would really serve to influence loyal football fans on their purchasing decisions and their loyalty levels, as football fans might not consider themselves as ordinary customers but as indirect owners of their supported teams (marketing a product to its owners seems to be a controversial approach, unless it aims at instigating a higher level of pride and emotional attachment to the brand/company), and also considering the other particularities of the sports' businesses domain. Therefore, it is worthwhile to have a deeper insight about traditional marketing concepts and its lack of relation with loyal football fans' reality.

In a simplistic way, one could say that marketing is concerned about making a product attractive enough in order to drive customer's attention and desire towards its consumption. According to Middleton & Clarke (2001, pp. 23), the British Chartered Institute of Marketing defines marketing as *"The management process responsible for identifying, anticipating and satisfying customer requirements profitably, to meet organizational objectives"*. Morrison et al (1999), highlight that the main idea in the marketing concept is that of satisfying customers with an innovative or better way. Palmer (1998) considers that within the definition of marketing orientation there are three important components, which are: the customer orientation, the competitor orientation and the inter-functional co-ordination which lies amongst the different levels of an organization such as HRM and operations, for instance. Similarly, Middleton & Clarke (2001) pinpoint some key elements of the marketing orientation which are resumed as follows: innovation and competitive attitude, satisfaction of customers and selective development of relationships and loyal buyers, profits and other organizational goals generated through customers' satisfaction and retention, awareness of competitors, continuing business development considering social and environmental constraints. From the marketing orientation derive the marketing techniques such as market research, advertising, pricing strategy, ways of distributing, motivation and control of personnel and product development; they all compose the marketing mix - such mix is also known as the 4 or 7Ps concept (Christopher et al 2002; Hoffman & Bateson, 2002; Gummesson, 2002; Middleton & Clarke, 200; Thomas, 1998; Palmer, 1998).

Hoffman & Bateson (2002) affirm that because of the intangibility trait of service products the traditional goods-related marketing mix cannot be applied in the former sector, as a cluster of different problems arise from this fact. Also, they state that by narrowing definitions about themselves, companies are put under the risk of applying the wrong marketing strategies, which would lead them to what some authors call the 'marketing myopia', resulting in a poor managerial performance. This concept is also emphasized by Glynn & Barnes (1995) when they refer to Gummesson's (1987) suggestion about the replacement of old marketing concept needs in order to avoid a 'myopic behaviour' in services businesses. Considering the main characteristics of a service (intangibility, inseparability, variability, perishability), Davidoff (1994) suggests some laws of service to be taken into account by service managers in order to better performance; these laws are related to customers' satisfaction, expectations and perceptions of a service. Palmer (1998) says that, although traditionally the marketing mix is composed by 4Ps (Product, Price, Promotion and Place), when it comes to services those components seem not to suffice the demanding nature of a service product and its consumers and therefore, an extended concept of marketing mix including new elements such as people, physical evidence and processes is needed - this constitutes the 7Ps concept of the Services Marketing Mix.

Another concept of marketing has emerged within management literature and it is named as Relationship Marketing (Gummesson, 2002; Christopher & Ballantyne, 2002). It is based upon the belief that the old 4 or 7Ps frameworks are not enough anymore to provide marketers with appropriate tools in order to cover all aspects related to the services sectors and their particularities. Also, it considers that companies must have a concern about customer's retention and loyalty if they want to stay in the present fluctuating and competitive market. Instead of 4 or 7Ps as the mainstream in marketing, Gummesson's (2002) suggests a 30Rs approach, which includes aspects such as internal customers relationship (concerned about the communication process within a company) and the service encounter (related to the contact between customers and a company). Table 1 below shows in a simple way the points covered by this 30Rs approach.

1. The thirty relationships of RM - the 30Rs (Gummesson, 2002).

Classic market relationships

R1 - Relationship between the supplier and the customer

R2 - The drama of the customer-supplier-competitor triangle

R3 - Distribution channels

Special market relationship

R4 - Relationships via full-time marketers and part-time marketers

R5 - The service encounter

R6 - The many-headed customer and many headed supplier

R7 - The relationship to the costumer's customer

R8 - The close versus the distant relationship

R9 - The relationship to the dissatisfied customer

R10 - The monopoly relationship

R11 - The customer as a 'member'

R12 - The e-relationship

R13 - Parasocial relationships

R14 - The non-commercial relationship

R15 - The green relationship

R16 - The law-based relationship

R17 - The criminal network

Mega relationships

R18 - Personal and social networks

R19 - Mega marketing

R20 - Alliances change the market mechanisms

R21 - The knowledge relationship

R22 - Mega alliances change the basic conditions for marketing

R23 - The mass media relationship

R24 - Market mechanisms are brought inside the company

R25 - Internal customer relationships

R26 - Quality and customer orientation

R27 - Internal marketing

R28 - The two-dimensional matrix relationship

R29 - The relationship to external providers of marketing services

R30 - The owner and financier relationship

The relationship marketing theory can be considered as being a more comprehensive marketing approach that vehemently emphasizes the importance of relationships not only amongst customers and companies and internal relationships within an organization, but also between different companies. Accordingly, much has been emphasized within marketing literature about the importance of building strategies to bolster customers' retention and loyalty through a continuing relationship among suppliers and customers in order to create an advantage for both parties; also, that each contact with the customers can be an opportunity to develop relationships (Gumesson, 2002; Sullivan & Adcock, 2002; Stone, Woodock & Machtynger, 2000; Lumsdon, 1997). Recently this new marketing concept has been applied in sports' marketing realm, as pinpointed by Kelley et al (1999). This trend in sports environment seems to have its basis on the fact that traditional marketing approaches do not suffice to address issues related to sports fans' attitude and behaviour and supporting this affirmation, Mullin et al. (2000: pp. 9) affirms that:

> "If sport marketing ideally consists of activities designed to meet the wants and needs of sport consumers, then historically the industry has been guilty of what Theodore Levitt called "marketing myopia" or "lack of foresight in marketing ventures"".

The authors point out some symptoms of this myopia as being: a focus on producing and selling rather than satisfying consumers; winning as the main marketing tool of a club; confusion between promotions and marketing; a shortsighted focus on short-term returns and lack of market research. These ideas are underpinned by the current research and also it is here believed that loyal football fans can by no means be seen as ordinary consumers because of their high level of emotional attachment and loyalty to their teams (Tapp & Clowes, 2000). Therefore, traditional marketing strategies also used in sport marketing seem not be enough to cover sports fans' (in the present case, football fans) particularities and this idea is going to be better debated next.

According to Morrison et al (1999), a new business/product must be attractive enough to convince a sufficient number of customers to spend their money on it. Palmer (1998) highlights that positioning is a marketing strategy which is used by an organization to differentiate its products, thus creating a market advantage - from these concepts it is possible to highlight some peculiarities which emphasizes the blurring terrain of the football fans' realm, as most of the loyal supporters may choose a specific team to bolster not because of marketing promotion strategies (unless in the case of franchising (Kelly et al, 1999); however, it has not happened yet within the football domain), but for reasons utterly unrelated to environmental and external appeals. Moreover, positioning and segmentation of football clubs in most of the cases are not the result of marketing research or other tools, but merely for social and historical motives.

Hoffman and Bateson (2002) point out that the customers' perception of value is not only based upon *'monetary costs'*, but also on *'time costs'*, *'energy cos*ts' and *'physic costs'*. The degree of cost will inextricably be dependent on customers' level of perception and expectation (Davidoff, 1994) of the service or product provided - in the football market the same concept can be applied, however, in a different fashion as in many cases the four types of costs above described might not be an obstacle (no matter how high they are) for football fans to support their teams even in times of bad clubs' performance, which makes the understanding of these consumers' perception of value and quality even more confusing in this case. Furthermore, independently of the degree of fans' expectations it still may not be a reason for them not to attend a match, as what may be of importance for a loyal football fan is their supportive presence in stadium or the benefits of such social experience.

The other three elements of the marketing mix concept, people, process and physical evidence can well be identified in the football market, although again in a different fashion from ordinary businesses. It is clear that without people a football club would not exist, however it is as far is it goes in similarity to other types of service businesses, as people (fans) have a different way of seeing their relationship with clubs/teams from the way they see it with a cinema theatre business, for instance. The process concept is also similar to other service businesses, however, the outcome of a service provided may not influence a post-purchasing decision as football loyal fans are highly emotionally involved with their supported teams and therefore, their zone of tolerance becomes quite wide towards their team - also, the feeling of belonging to an entity and of loyalty to that entity will be enough to motivate a fan to go to another match, as again what would be of importance for them is their supportive presence also in clubs' difficult times; without mentioning the benefits of the social experience itself. The physical evidence may help to increase football fans' pride and satisfaction and Wakefield & Blodgett (1994) cited by Theodorakis et al. (2001) had already emphasized the influence of servicescape on spectators' sports satisfaction. However, there is no evidence of which sports modality they were talking about and moreover, no evidence of whether generalizations were made for all sport modalities (considering that each sports modality has a different context and has different fan's attitudes and behaviour towards it). In the case of football, the author of the present research argues that servicescape ought not to be a detrimental factor for loyal fans' decision to support a team or buy its products, given their emotional involvement with the team. Finally and to add in complexity, even if a club delivers a service or product with high quality (e.g. wins most of the matches played) it could hinder supporters' attendance to matches as the predictability of results may well decrease fans' excitement as well as willingness to go to stadium, unless they had other reasons to attend a match.

According to Sullivan & Adcock (2002), it is easier to retain a satisfied customer than to attract a new one, however it does not always mean repeat purchases. They suggest that in order for a customer to be loyal to a specific business an emotional involvement must take place in addition to an economic benefit - in the football fans' (customers) domain it may be true that satisfaction with their teams performance will increase the probability of match attendance, although it is not the main condition for stadium's high attendance, as it has been seen in other sports modalities such as baseball where even with the case of a long-term team's losses, supporters of the Chicago Cubs remained loyal to their team and the average match attendance has even increased (Bristow & Sebastian, 2001). It is here believed that it can well be the same case in football as well.

As mentioned above, in order to become loyal, a person needs to feel an emotional involvement with someone or something and the same concept applies for football clubs/fans' relationships. However, non-fan customers' loyalty cannot be seen the same as football fans loyalty, as the latter will probably have their main reason to be loyal a high emotional attachment to their team with commercial benefits not even being considered an issue; furthermore, this feeling of attachment is probably related to the social group that the team supported represents (which might have an important symbolic signification to football fans - this issue will be addressed in the next chapter) and not to the business organization behind it. In addition, other elements such as the total uncertainty of outcomes of the product purchased by a football fan (consumer) and the psychological effects involved in the product delivery process will be determinant to drift apart the concepts of loyalty in goods-related and service businesses and in the sports realm - because of the uncertainty of outcomes in sports is a fundamental element for fans' enjoyment and involvement, it provokes a decrease in fans' expectations, which can be another reason for their high zone of tolerance.

Mason (1999) and Hunt et al (1999) emphasize that sports' fans very often engage in a practice known as Basking in Reflected Glory (BIRG) or Cutting-off Reflected Failure (CORF) according to the performance of their supported team - this suggests that fans express their discontent or satisfaction with the product purchased in a very much personalized and emotionally internalized way which may or not cause temporary dissociation with the clubs supported. However, in the case of loyal football fans, such dissociation seems not to happen, as this type of fans seem to suffer their team's loss as a personal failure - a non-fan customer would react in a completely different fashion if, for instance, a different purchased entertainment did not suffice its expected level of quality. The idea of the existence of differences between non-fan consumers' and fans' attitudes and traits is supported also by the findings of Sebastian & Bristow's research (2000) cited by Bristow & Sebastian (2001), where they found out that the lack of quality of a product provided such as clothes, soft drinks, tennis shoes, and delivered pizza, was a reason for a decrease in brand loyalty by college students, whereas no negative impact were shown in brand loyalty when professional sports' teams did not offer a good product quality or high performance to the same students surveyed.

All this indicates that marketing approaches within sports field ought to be bettered and more case specific, starting from the fact that there must be a relationship and certain differences between the level of loyalty and the level of tolerance of loyal sports fans with football fans making no exception in this case. Furthermore, understanding the real reasons of devoted sports/football fans to become and remain loyal to their teams is the first step for the development of more precise marketing approaches. Conclusively, the remaining question is really why and how this high level of loyalty and tolerance of football fans towards their teams emerges and is sustained throughout life.

As it has been pointed out already, there seems to be differences between the emotional attachment towards a brand of non-fan and fan customers, or even more believed here, that emotional attachment towards a good/services related brand is not a common phenomenon (Bristow &

Sebastian, 2001) and therefore cannot even be compared with the emotional attachment that loyal sports fans show towards their teams (in this case, football fans). Moreover, the level of loyalty and the width of the tolerance zone of loyal football fans, for instance, ought to have origins and justification other than in pure commercial benefits amongst customers and businesses. Therefore, a better understanding about human attitude and social attachment and about the social paradigm which society is at present based upon becomes fundamental before any attempt to explore the loyal football fans' domain take place, as no social phenomenon can be dissociated from its social context and from its individuals' holistic traits. In addition, another factor that has to be considered is that there will be different levels of loyalty amongst football fans of the same team as well as their zone of tolerance will vary accordingly. These issues will be better addressed in the next chapter.

A multidimensional postmodern social perspective of football fans

To have a deeper comprehension about what triggers human attitude and behaviour, it is worthwhile to look at the definitions of attitude in order to better understand human behaviour and its passivity to external influential factors. However, it would not be possible to talk about human attitude without first addressing the concept of symbolic interaction, which according to Jones and Day cited by Hendrich (1977) is the attempt of an individual to interpret and understand their surroundings. They emphasise that symbolic interaction is not a characteristic of infancy but it exists throughout the process of human beings' maturation with a continuing construction of reality. Hendrich (1977) affirms that equally important to symbolic interaction is communication and that without communication human beings would not be able to share their experiences and perceptions of reality, but also that human communication process happens through an exchange of symbols.

According to Krech & Crutchfield (1928) cited by Kiesler et al (1969), attitude is the intensity of a positive or a negative individual's affection towards or against a psychological object with the latter being described as any symbol, person, phrase or idea.

Attitude can be considered as a set of psychological elements such as motivation, emotion, perception and cognitive process in combination and is related to the individual's world, leading to responsiveness to the environment. Taking into consideration the statement above, it is already clear that the level of affection intensity of an individual towards an idea or symbol, for instance, will depend upon the personal signification that those elements possess for that individual. Considering the influence of postmodernism in society, it is possible to say that the concept of symbol and idea are passive of change and of meaning variation. If symbol can be distorted or modified in meaning in postmodernist society, the individual's perception (signification) of it will be consequently compromised as well as their cognitive process, which consequently will lead to a modification of an individual's communication process, thus, influencing the affection intensity for or against psychological objects, in other words, influencing human attitude. Therefore, it is not wrong to speculate that football fans' attitude towards their teams can be also passive of this influence. A deeper analysis about postmodernism will be addressed later in this chapter.

Another human psychological aspect that is inextricably related to human attitude and it is important to be considered here is the social attachment, which according to Hendrich (1977) has implications for the behaviour of an organism towards the object of attachment and possibly everything else - although this statement is based upon research on animals there are some evidences that social attachments in humans might be analogous to the attachment patterns of lower animals. Theories of social behaviour are based upon the fact the organisms influence each other and in order to do so they need to be in proximity, which means that within a group individual's interactions are an indispensable element for the construction of social reality. If individuals' interactions within a group influence each other, consequently social attachment is passive of this influence as well as culture and social environment, and also other values such as loyalty. For instance, in a research about brand loyalty towards the Chicago Cubs baseball team, Bristow & Sebastian (2001) show that the high level of fans' loyalty towards a team can considerably be influenced by relatives/parents and surroundings throughout childhood.

Considering what has already been said about symbolic interaction and attitude, it is possible to reach the conclusion that there exist social icons which for persons have more symbolic importance than others, thus the affection towards psychological objects within society also vary accordingly as well as social attachment. Football clubs can be considered one of the many psychological objects that have different levels of signification for people from the same social background and this implies that the level of affection and attachment to a specific club will vary according to personal signification given to such organisation. According to Gwinner & Swanson (2003), the degree of involvement of fans with a given team can vary and this variation will be influenced by the way a fan identifies themselves with such team - based on these arguments, one can say that by consequence the level of football fans' loyalty and zone of tolerance again will be variable accordingly.

As most of the football clubs tend to represent a specific geographic area even if in the same city there are more the one team, for instance; and since they had their beginning from small social initiatives (e.g. a group of friends within a local community) they become a benchmark for social identification, pertaining and attachment. Therefore, it is coherent to ascertain that the explanations for football fans' loyalty and their zone of tolerance can be based on social reasons associated with psychological elements such as social identification and self-esteem – Interestingly, this idea is in accordance with the three fundamental components that contribute to consumer's brand loyalty offered by Sheth et al (1999) cited by Bristow & Sebastian (2001), which are: social and emotional identification with a brand and habit and long history with such brand.

It is already clear that the present study is very much based upon the social identity theory which lays its main argument in the fact that an individual classifies themselves into different social categories in order to enable a better self-definition within their social environment (Asforth & Mael, 1989). Social identification is determined by an individual's choice for their relation and linkage to social groups and it is the premise for social interaction and participation. It is assumed that the perception of belonging to a specific social group leads to an enhancement of self-esteem (Hogg & Turner, 1985; Tajfel, 1978) and it can be said therefore, by consequence, of an individuals' emotional attachment.

A social group can be defined, as an aggregate of people who share similar beliefs, traditions and lifestyle, and therefore the affirmation that sports fans' groupings can be considered one of the many variations of social groupings is pertinent. If a team can be considered as a form of psychological object, team identification is beyond doubt possible. This will consequently lead to a formation of social bound/group. Complementally, Gwinner & Swanson (2003) say that team identification is defined as the spectators' perception of personal connectedness to a team supported and the feeling of ownership derived from this relation and expressed by the predisposition of a fan to share their teams' failings and achievements as their own. Congruently, the high level of football fan's loyalty and tolerance is here believed to being determined by the feeling of ownership they have towards their teams. Additionally, important for the research here proposed, social identity theory suggests that people who identify with organisations (in this case, a football club) will engage in activities to bolster the latter (Ashforth & Mael, 1989).

From another perspective, given the changes in the present society and in social values by the influence of postmodernism, one could argue that emotional attachment and personal team identification and connectedness to it would be passive of such social paradigm and that it would compromise therefore their sustainability. By consequence, football fans' loyalty feelings and attitude could by all means suffer similar impact. Counter arguing such belief however, the influence of external factors such a social paradigm is here believed not to be a determinant for attitude pattern changes of devoted football fans, because the emotional bound between supporters and their teams and amongst themselves would overcome such external pressures anyway.

The concept of postmodernism as a social paradigm is as complex as its own existence at the present time. There are controversies regarding its existence, but there also are indications that traces of it can be identified through expressions in many areas such as academic disciplines, philosophy, architecture, film studies, literature, music, fashion, sexuality and so forth (Connor, 2001; Jameson, 1995; Smart, 1993). According to Jameson (1995), culture itself has become a product in post-modernist society and there is a natural tendency of *'aestheticization'* of reality. In postmodernist society, every possible way of expression is either extremely acceptable or purely rejected; chaos becomes part of everyday life and a disorder of 'things' take place as well as a social commodification process. Whilst Modernism looked forward to the coming future, Postmodernism looks for moments to be lived now, because later they could not have the same meaning (Jameson, 1995). In post-modernist society there is a constant alternation of states that allows the old to become new and vice versa, and contradictions and intersections of ideas exist contemporarily.

"The post-modern condition, we are told repeatedly, manifests itself in the multiplication of centres of power and activity and the dissolution of every kind of totalising narrative which claims to govern the whole complex field of social activity and representation" *(Connor, 2001).*

Smart (1993) highlights that there is a relationship between postmodernism and what he calls *'the erosion of cultural hierarchies'*, the concern about new technologies and the spread of consumerism. He also cites post-modernity as a way of living with doubts, uncertainties, anxieties, price to be paid in order to gain in return, the benefits and the pleasures related to post-modernity. It is not necessary to carry out a scientific research to realise some of these social elements of the depiction above offered. Moreover, it is possible to conclude that this new paradigm ought to have a powerful influence on the way human beings act in today's society.

Based on the assumption of the post-modernism impact on society, Morrison et al (1999) points out the concept of *'post-modernist consumer challenge'* which is related to the transition of customers' traits, from straightforward to extremely heterogeneous, open to the new and behaviourally volatile. Cova & Sevenfold (1993) cited by Morrison et al (1999) affirm that post-modernist individuals are free to choose what is most suitable to suffice their whims, which in turn leads to what they call a 'general promiscuity and playful mixing of codes'; they also affirm that it might well be possible that a post-modernist consumer assumes similar behavioural patterns. Within this context Gumesson (2002) affirms that in post-modernist society companies can be suppliers, customers and competitors as well as they can own one another; he emphasises that the advancements in technology, biological sciences, and innovations such as deregulation and privatisation have been modifying the actual social reality. There is no doubt about the complexity of the current market and the difficulty that marketing professionals have been having to attract customers to purchase not only new, but also existing products and even more to apply traditional marketing principles and strategies within the sports fans' domain, as this segment can subdivided into "micro segments" according to the types of fans existent in the sports market.

Based upon the arguments presented above, it is assumable that postmodernism can influence symbol perception and as symbol perception influences motivation, cognition and communication process will also suffer similar impact; thus, culture is also modified, and consequently it will influence human attitude and emotional attachment capability. Interestingly, it seems to be that football fans' loyal attitude towards their supported teams has not been changing by the influence of this post-modernist shake-up. However, it is possible to say that with the globalisation process extremely influenced by a commercial mentality and TV broadcasting, football teams widened their domain also abroad gaining fans adherence where least expected, as in the case of Israeli fans of British teams such as Manchester United and Arsenal (Ben-Porat, 2000) and the Irish following for English football (Mason, 1999) - this phenomenon goes against the belief that loyal fans might be motivated by a deep social identification with their teams. Nevertheless, long-term supporters have remained loyal to their current teams or at least it is unknown that a chaotic exchange of fans support between different clubs has been taking place recently. Therefore, from this perspective it is likely that football fans' loyalty has its origin based on elements other than just the benefit-related relationship found in common business transactions;

these elements are here believed to be social elements such as the need

for interaction and socialisation.

According to the Chambers Concise Dictionary (1991), loyal can be

defined as: faithful, firm in allegiance, personally devoted to a sovereign,

government, etc - this definition implies that a person must believe in

something that is symbolically valuable for them and does not have

rational justification, but it is justified purely by faith. Taking into

consideration the assumption that loyalty is inextricably dependent upon

symbolic interpretation of a person, and that one through this process

identifies themselves and interacts within a specific group with a certain

level of affection; then, that would not be much presumption to affirm

that there exists a close relationship between loyalty and emotional

attachment, as the latter could not happen without the former elements

and vice versa. In other words, there is no loyal behaviour towards a

person or cause if there is no personal identification with those elements,

and given that personal identification cannot exist without a social context (a social group) and social attachment, emotional attachment in this case becomes absent also. Thus, loyalty and emotional attachment have very similar meanings, if they are not synonyms within social context. In the case of devoted football fans, it seems that these elements are not modified by the influence of postmodernism.

It is already evident that loyalty has a close relation with emotional attachment and/or bound to something, which can be an ideology or a body, for instance. McGoldrick and Andre (1997) cited by Sullivan & Adcock (2002) affirm that elements such as affection, fidelity or commitment are inextricably linked to the concept of loyalty; therefore, in order to develop loyal behaviour it is essential that a person be emotionally involved in a relationship. In the case of a relationship between a business and a customer it becomes quite unclear whether such feelings of affection or attachment can be achieved in today's society, especially amongst globalised giant corporations and non-fan consumers. Moreover, with so many options available in the market one could doubt that a person would hold a favourable attitude towards a specific brand, unless a positive reward is to be gained (it could be a financial or a psychological one) - even though, it is possible to predict that a person would switch their loyalty as soon as such reward is withdrawn or another offer from a competitor overcomes the previous reward benefits. As a conclusion, non-fan customers' loyalty seems to be a rare phenomenon nowadays (Bristow & Sebastian, 2001). Alternatively, it could be said that either the concept of loyalty cannot coexist with the concept of trade or the way marketers apply the current marketing approaches is wrong – one could say that they have certainly been used unilaterally or myopically (Mullin et al, 2000) in the sports field.

However, loyalty towards sports teams (it could be also called sports brands) does exist indeed and if the motives for this to happen were understood, it would be possible then to develop marketing approaches in order to boost even more football fans' loyalty and their active participation in their club's 'business' transactions. There exist findings from researches that point to the belief that an inside-fans-domain approach can be fruitful on the search for understanding better sports fans' attitude and behaviour, and consequently to develop ways to motivate them to engage more actively in supporting activities towards their teams (Gwinner & Swanson, 2003; Hunt et al, 1999).

Congruent to this perspective, Cova & Cova (2002) offer a different vision of marketing approach that is based upon the *Latin School of Societing* which has as its leitmotif: *'the link is more important than the thing'* and which help to better understand the inspiration for the research here proposed. They emphasise the idea of the tribalisation of post-modern society, and the tribal marketing concept instead of the Northern concept of society, which is mainly based upon individualism. As these authors (pp. 599) point out:

> *"In a Latin approach (Club de Marseille, 1994; Maffesoli, 1996a), society resembles a network of*

societal micro-groups, in which individuals share strong emotional links, a common subculture, a vision of life. In our times, these micro-groups develop their own complexes of meanings and symbols and form more or less stable tribes, which are invisible to the categories of sociology. Each individual belongs to several tribes, in each of which he might play a different role and wear a different mask; this means that the rational tools of sociological analysis cannot classify him. And belonging to a social class or segment. The social status, that is to say the static position of an individual in one of the social classes, is progressively replaced by the societal configuration, that is to say the dynamic and flexible positioning of the individual within and between his tribes".

Marketing in this perspective seeks to find the reasons why people gather together or choose different tribes to join in; it searches information from inside these "tribes" becoming part of them or using their members to understand what bind them together, to understand their links and motives instead of offering something new to the market that may not have any relation to tribal beliefs, and which would be a disastrous idea to attract tribal consumers anyway. This perspective shows a promising understanding of how to achieve true relationship marketing and also how to develop a sense of brand loyalty in non-fan consumers' domain. Regarding football fans, as said before, it would be difficult to apply the ordinary marketing approaches in the field, given the fact that what motivates these fans to purchase a product (a ticket for a game, for instance) ought not to be the mutual commercial benefits of it, but intrinsic elements that are inextricably related to the concept of tribes - therefore, the 'tribal marketing' concept seems to be a suitable tool for the loyal football fans' field. Cova & Cova (2002) highlight that a tribe is defined as a network of heterogeneous people who are related by a shared emotion or passion; that these same people can act collectively for a specific motive and therefore they cannot be seen as ordinary consumers, but also as advocates. Moreover, the authors affirm that rituals are the form tribes have to express their shared beliefs and social belonging and that example of these rituals can include specific clothing, magical or ritual words, idols, icons, etc. Such a definition could not draw a better picture of loyal football fans.

Therefore, the assumption taken in this study that football fans' loyalty has its origin based on elements other than common commercial benefits exchange is extremely plausible and it finds its foundation on the assumption that these feelings of loyalty come from social elements such as the interaction amongst persons and mutual influence that people from the same geographic area and cultural background or even tribes have, associated with a deep emotional attachment to their social 'clans' and teams. Furthermore, by the influence of emotional attachment, other psychological aspects such as pride for belonging to a specific group, region and nation and so forth also emerge; this in turn, will even more considerably diminish the possibility for a football fan to switch their loyalty to another club only for the sake of financial or materialistic benefits. Such affirmation goes against the assumption of Ben-Porat (2000) who assumes that fans' relationship with their clubs have the same elements found in ordinary customers/businesses relationship, and therefore both can be said to be comparable. Moreover, he suggests that a fan can choose different teams again and again to suffice their demand for personal benefits. Contradictorily, the same author using the concept of "reference group" (Merton, 1949) affirm that because a club serve as a reference group for a committed fan some aspects of their behaviour as an individual are influenced by that given club. Furthermore, Ben-Porat did not consider the differences in loyalty levels amongst fans.

Given the fact that fans' level of loyalty and tolerance towards clubs supported by them are variable, it is evident that there exist different types of fans, as it already has been suggested within sports marketing literature (Gwinner & Swanson, 2003; Tapp & Clowes, 2002; Bristow &

Sebastian, 2001; Hunt et al, 1999, Mason, 1999). Gwinner & Swanson (2003) offer a three-potential influences model (perceived prestige, domain involvement, fan associations) which is related to team identification and may be a way to understand the reasons why a fan identifies with a specific social group (in this case a football team). Although the model does not directly typify fans, it offers insights that can serve as the basis for explanations about different levels of fans' loyalty. Bristow & Sebastian (2001), start from the notion that the highest level of loyalty is found in the *"die-hard"* classification of fans and that according to the influence of other factors such as social and emotional brand identification, the level of loyalty may decrease or increase. A specific classification offered by Hunt et al (1999) seems to quite precisely describe the various types of fans, although such model should not be seen as exhaustive and should carefully be applied outside the terrain where the research has been carried out, as differences between fans of different sports modalities and socio-cultural factors can determine people's attitude, behaviour and conception of reality. Nonetheless, it can undoubtedly serve as a benchmark for other research initiatives. Their model is divided into 5 categories of fans and they are as follows: the temporary fan, the local fan, the devoted fan, the fanatical fan and the dysfunctional fan. It is worthwhile to go through these definitions as they offer a good representation of sports fans' domain.

The temporary fans consist in those people who follow a time-specific event and therefore their loyalty vanishes when such event ends. - A good example of them is people who are interested only in major events such as the Olympics or the Football World Cup. The local fans are those who relate to a geographic-specific team or event because of their social bonds to a specific place where, for instance, could be their birthplace. The devoted fans are those who are not under time and location constraints and remain loyal even in times of their teams' hardship - the high level of identification with an object is the main reason why such fans have a high level of loyalty, which is inextricably related to the influence a given team has on supporters, and which in addition serves as instrument to strengthen supporters' self-concept. The fanatical fan share similarities with the devoted fan, although the former shows a very high level of self-identification with their team and engage in a fan-like behaviour up to the point of dressing up in a funny way and exposing themselves to ridicule - which is not a problem for such fans. The dysfunctional fans are those who are not really interested in the game itself but seek for trouble and behave in a violent fashion; they use the team supported as a way of distinguishing themselves from others, and being a fan plays an important role on their lives, if it is not the central aspect of their lives - this type of fans are extremely dangerous and can damage the image of the sport itself; a good example of them are the "Hooligans". The problem with such classification is that when it comes to differentiate devoted from fanatical fans it becomes a blurred task, as it is not certain that a devoted fan would not behave in a similar fashion as the fanatical ones, given that their reasons to be loyal come from the same origins; moreover, to typify fans does not solve the problem of identifying them amongst one another. Finally, the concept of dysfunctional fan is more related to social maladjustment than to social identity theories and therefore they should not be classified as sports fans. Nonetheless, the devoted fan classification seems to offer a good basis for the present research to determine the definition of loyal fan to be used later in data sampling process.

Tapp & Clowes (2002), in their study about segmentation in sports market, propose a fan classification that is quite similar to the one offered by Hunt et al. (1999), although their definition about the fanatical type of fans is more related to the dysfunctional one of Hunt et al (1999). They classify fans based on a series of perspectives and some of them are highlighted next. One of the classifications divides fans into three categories according to the value fans have to clubs: Fanatics, Regular and Casuals (this category is subdivided into "carefree" and "committed" casual fans). Then, the same authors point out another 6-type classification, which relates to product need. Unfortunately, at the end, they did not recommend any practical solution for the problem of how to achieve marketing segmentation in the sports field and remained on explaining how to delimitate market segments based upon the different types of fans. In addition, some of their classifications are controversial such as the concept of "football" and "club" fans, where the former is related to those fans that identify with the entertainment product (therefore, they are less loyal than the "club" fan) and the latter are those who identify with the clubs. It is an valuable idea, however, either types above described must identify with the entertainment product anyway, otherwise they would not be considered sports fans; moreover "football" fans, by indirect relation, must identify with clubs (even if they are from a specific league), as entertainment without clubs' existence would not be possible (perhaps the difference between this two categories lays on the fact that "football" are "polygamist" loyal fans, whereas "club" fans are "monogamist" loyal). Finally, the fact that one states that they identify more with the entertainment product than with a club does not mean that the same person cannot consider themselves to be loyal to a specific club and does not act according to their beliefs.

Although the fan classifications suggested by such researches are an important contribution for the understanding of the different types and levels of fan's loyalty, other constraining problems for marketers still remain, such as how to identify whether within the same type of fans there exist differences of loyalty level and how to segment them within the football market. Finding the solutions for such problems are far from being the intention of the present research, as it does neither presume to fully explain the endless variables involved in the football fans' domain nor wants it to address such variables in a simplistic way. Therefore, as in any other academic research, it aims at understanding a small portion of a complex phenomenon, a specific type of football fan who falls into the very similar classifications offered by Bristow & Sebastian (2001) - the "die-hard" fan; and Hunt et al (1999) - the "devoted" fan, to contribute with new knowledge in order to help to understanding about the intrinsic motives for the high level of loyalty and tolerance of this specific type of fans.

Inasmuch as what has been said; it is no presumption to affirm that the use of marketing approaches should be adapted to the reality of each different sports modality and also within the same modality as each of them have subgroups of different types of fans. Only through an emphasis on understanding fans' motives (in the present case, devoted football fans) to become loyal to a specific team, sports marketers will be able to develop more case-specific strategies to act effectively in this complex market terrain. By finding out such motives, it would possible to understand why the zone of tolerance of devoted Football fans is high. In addition, from such findings it may be possible to improve or even develop marketing strategies to exploit such elements related to devoted football fans' justifications for their loyalty to encourage them to become even more loyal to their teams and, possibly, to encourage them to engage in a word of mouth process in order to convince other less loyal fans of the benefits of becoming a devoted fan. Moreover, such findings would help marketers to promote the emergence of new-devoted fans.

The Approach

This research has its focus on devoted football fans only, given the importance football has around the world and because to date this field has been little scientifically explored. Not mentioning the social importance of football as a business.

Given the fact that there exist different types of fans according to their level of loyalty towards their clubs supported, this research took one male participant classified as a "devoted" fan (Hunt et al, 1999) - The devoted fans are those who are not under time and location constraints and remain loyal even in times of their teams' hardship - the high level of identification with an object is the main reason why such fans have a high level of loyalty, which is inextricably related to the influence a given team has on supporters and additionally serves as instrument to strengthen supporters' self-concept. To avoid misuse of term and misunderstandings, the author mainly used the classification "devoted" fan offered by Hunt et al (1999). The number of participants was limited to only one, because (for the research design (qualitative) and approach (case study) here chosen) of time and financial resource constraints, which unfortunately did not enable a wider sampling to obtain more comprehensive information in order to offer an even deeper insight. Nonetheless, such deterrents did not lessen this research importance as the number of participants is not a constraint for qualitative research. It can be done even with a "N" as small as 1 (Padgett, 1998). Hence, because this work was based on qualitative approach, it did not seek statistical significance through a numerically representative sampling and findings. Instead, the objective here was to have a deep analysis of the phenomena "devoted" football fans, starting from the expectation of discovering and analyzing what the research participant understands about himself and considering the social context he was inserted in.

The instrument applied for data gathering was a 'semi standardized' interview (Berg, 2001) and the strategy used for sampling was the *purposive* one (Padgett, 1998), as the author already knew a Man United's supporter that fell into the classification of "devoted" fan. Also, the research can be considered reliable as the football fan interviewed did not live in Manchester but in Leyland - Lancashire, which characterizes the concept of "devoted" fan that are not under time and location constraints and remain loyal even in times of their teams' hardship. Due to a previous visit to his home it has been clear that there are other strong signs of high level of fan's loyalty as the participant is a season ticket holder, follows all matches of Man United on cable TV when he cannot attend a match in the stadium, and possess a big collection of Man United magazines and other memorabilia. Moreover, the participant is a committed Catholic that goes to masses every Sunday and even belongs to the pastoral council of the parish (PPC). However, in times when there are decisive matches for Man United, the participant is ready to miss a Mass or even a PPC meeting for the sake of supporting his team. In addition, the participant has been supporting Man United for the last 30 years missing only four of all home games during this period of time. Finally, including a participant of a family that values sports in the sampling and data gathering process allowed the researcher to analyse elements such as family influence on the process of choosing a team to support, also because the father of the research's participant does not support Man United F.C. and even prefer rugby to football. The participant chosen can be classified as a person from middle class family, being male and at age of 60. The researcher has met the participant through his work at the Leyland St. Mary´s Catholic parish and although the participant cannot be considered a close friend, there has been enough disclosure and trusting between him and the researcher to assure that sound and reliable data were gathered.

The interview has taken place at Leyland St. Mary's Priory. A voice recorder has been used as the data collection tool and a previous questions' guideline for the interview has been prepared in advance. That was mainly to assure that the interview covered areas related to the research theoretical body and that the procedures and attitude of the researcher did not overlook ethical issues and did not deviate in any other way from the purposes of the research. The data gathering had its ending when it reached enough saturation in needed information, which was characterized by the redundancy of data. Finally, the participant agreed with having more the one interview session and have made himself available in case it was necessary (Berg, 2001).

The data analysis approach applied here was the interpretive one with the *latent content* analysis being used as its technique, as a *manifest content* would not be viable in this case for the number of participants of this research. The data analysis was based on three concurrent steps: the data reduction, display and conclusions/verification, and during its process themes and paragraphs were used as units of analysis (Berg, 2001). In order for that to happen, a previous data management took place with the interview's entries being recorded with specified date, time and place. The participant did not have his name revealed but, instead, he has been identified by the code "A" in order to protect the confidentiality of information given by him and his anonymity (Berg, 2001). Straight after the interview, the data collected was transcribed and stored on computer and memory stick - this process other than guaranteeing the non-loss of important information for lack of attention of the interviewer, it also feedbacked the researcher's performance during the interview process, helping to immediately identify possible mistakes made.

After data transcription, the data coding was the next step. The method of coding used here is the *constant comparative analysis,* a technique that according to Padgett (1998) is associated with grounded theory (Strauss & Corbin, 1990) and consists in an iterative process which starts from an inductive, goes through a deductive and returns to an inductive approach, finally relating the findings to existing scientific literature. *A line-by-line coding* seemed to be a useful needed strategy, even if the data gathered was from only one interviewee. Then, assumptions-related matrix groups were created based on groupings of excerpts from the interview with these serving as the basis for the creation of different themes that emerged during the inductive phase of the coding process and that was later related to the theoretical body of this study. The coding process was ended when repetition and redundancy began to appear, characterizing what is called *saturation* within literature (Padgett, 1998).

Five assumptions emerged from the interview's data:

1 - Devoted football fans do not see themselves as ordinary consumers but as 'indirect owners' and therefore their zone of tolerance (Lovelock & Wright, 2002; Groeroos, 2000) towards their team is high;

2 - The loyalty of devoted football fans to their teams starts from childhood because of family/peer influences;

3 - Devoted football fans have an emotional attachment to their teams for regional/community/social status or pride reasons;

4 - Tolerance and loyalty levels are reciprocally influential and can determine the attitude of devoted football fans towards the teams

supported by them;

5 – The consumerist and materialistic mentality of postmodernist society have not influenced the loyalty of devoted football fans.

More accurately, once the coding of excerpts from the interviews' transcription was finished and allocated into the different groups of data, themes were allocated into the assumptions' matrix groups and were used for the final steps of data analysis and the conclusions drawing process.

The universe of a devoted football fan

From the interview (18 questions) have derived substantial data and from them the themes and excerpts which were classified according to 5 assumptions deduced from the data gathering.

1 - How would you see yourself in your relationship with the club you support? Is it a close relationship? if yes, how would you describe it?

2 - Do you consider yourself a consumer of a service provider's product when you go to matches or sign up for exclusive cable TV broadcasting of your club's matches?

3 - So, then you consider yourself a customer, a consumer in this case?

4 - Do you think that your relationship with your club is pure commercial with both parties benefiting from it?

5 - What does it mean for you being loyal to someone/something or some cause or beliefs?

6 - Would you switch your loyalty to another club if your club does not suffice your performance expectations?

7 - How did you decide to support Man United?

8 - Why do you support Man United given that you don't live in Manchester? Have you ever lived in Manchester before?

9 - Do you see Man United as a representative of Lancashire Region? If yes, Why?

10 - Do you feel a connection to Man United for any social status reason?

11 - Do you think that Man United is a club for the rich only, nowadays?

12 - Are you proud of being a supporter of Man United? Why?

13 - Do you think that if you weren't so loyal to your team you would tolerate its lack of performance in competitions?

14 - Suppose it could be possible to predict that Man United would not qualify for the next 5 years, neither as champion nor within the three first places in all existing

competitions in England and Europe, would you still remain loyal to your team? If yes, why?

15 – Would you say that going to matches at present, also during these 30 years?, 20 years? (29 years)…Right, do you think that going to matches would be a way to experience again that first time you went to stadium?

16 – Do you think that going to matches is…could you say that the stadium and the match itself are a refuge from the world or some of the stressful things you have in your life or everything you would consider stressful or bad? Is it correct?

17 – So, do you think that the matches, the stadium, would be the only moment when you have time for

yourself? I mean, considering that you go on holiday with your family, this a break anyway from stress of life, but, I mean, only for you, because you don't have your family around you. So, would it be correct to say that?

18- Would you switch your loyalty to another team if it offered some sort of financial and/or status benefits?

The following interview's excerpts are related to assumption 1: devoted football fans do not see themselves as ordinary consumers but as "indirect owners" and therefore their zone of tolerance (Lovelock & Wright, 2002; Groenroos, 2000) towards their team is high.

Q1 excerpt lines 1- 4 and 4-9:

"I'm obviously very devoted to the club and very passionate, but my feelings are that the club doesn't know me even though I've been going there since 1975. I feel as a season ticket holder, I'm just another number or another phrase a "bum on the seat", so I don't think there's any relationship with the club."

"I tried to get some semi-finals tickets which I eventually got, but I was late applying for the semi-final tickets this season, and cup final tickets, so when I spoke to the club direct and explained that I'd been away for business they weren't prepared to make any compromise at all and treated me just as a number and therefore, I've no great affections for the management of the club, as a business or organization."

Q2 excerpt lines 1-2 and 4-7:

"I'm sometimes a little bit bitter about the commercial aspects of the club and I'll tend to avoid purchases at the club..."

"I do purchase a programme currently three pounds for every game and that's more of a tradition, but I do like to read the contents, I really like to read the manager's opinions and thoughts before a game rather than after a game, so I've also subscribed to the programme scape, but I feel no obligation to purchase additional things from the club."

Q3 excerpt lines 1-3 and 4:

"I'm a consumer or a customer because I purchase the season ticket every year and purchase the programmes. Yes, but I also won't be misguided, I also think I can see the minimum that I have to do to get the maximum out of the football team…"

"Cause it's the team, it's the football that I love, that I enjoy."

Q4 excerpt lines 1-3 and 6:

"Eh…both parties benefiting from it…I haven't really thought of it that way, before…yes, I suppose I'm purchasing a form of entertainment, and obviously I feel that it's value for money otherwise I wouldn't't be going."

"So, yes I'm getting advantage of the club."

Q5 excerpt lines 11-14 and 22-27:

"Ah...loyalty is a...I don't feel I can be loyal to the club, I feel I'm being more loyal to myself, if that's an appropriate phrase...I get so much enjoyment and pleasure out of the football and it's a big release from both family life, social upbringing and work stress point of view. I almost feel I've earned the right to go and therefore it's something I need as part of my routine."

"There's some loyalty with the team, as I don't change teams, I have never changed teams, but the benefits are for myself...being selfish...you know the enjoyment is purely for myself and therefore that I think it's probably one of the main reasons why I still continue to go and also think it helps from a family point of view that we have our own interests, both husband and wife, we share a little bit of interest in each other's hobbies etc., plus I give her some free time as well. So, it has for me also other benefits."

Q6 excerpt lines 6-11.

"…You know if I go back to the 80s we played some poor football, very poor football and the crowds were dropping significantly, from an average of 48.000 down to that of 35.000, but I would never consider not going, I'd still go, I'd get excited with the anticipation, I'd enjoy the match regardless of the result and no doubt mourn about it for the next two or three days, but I'd be back for the next game. So yes, there's a degree of loyalty."

Based on the comments of the interviewee it is possible to reach the conclusion that the affirmation about devoted football fans feeling as "indirect owners" has not found support in this particular case. It is clear that the participant sees his relationship with the club in a commercial way. Therefore, the relationship between the feelings of being "indirect owners" cannot be bolstered by such findings nor can it be said that such feelings have an influence on the width of the zone of tolerance of a devoted football fan. The findings, in this case, also do not support the assumption made by Gwinner & Swanson (2003) who affirm that team identification is defined as the spectators' perception of personal connectedness to a team supported, and that the feelings of ownership derived from this relation is expressed by the predisposition of a fan to consider their teams' failings and achievements as their own – it seems that it would be more precise to say that it is because of fan's loyalty feelings that they consider their teams' failings and achievements as their own and not because of ownership feelings, as suggested by those authors. In the case here studied, it seems that there are no ownership feelings deriving from his personal connectedness and team identification as well as his loyalty towards his team is not based on such feelings either.

This can be verified on questions 1, 2, 3 and 4.

An interesting information given by the interviewee was not expected by the author and it is when the interviewee on questions 1 lines 4-9, 2 lines 1-7 and 3 line 4 emphasizes the business side of the club and the fact that what he loves is the team, the football, which indicates that he separates his relationship with the club as a business organization and with the football team as something that he is emotionally involved with - despite the fact that he sometimes he uses the noun "club" to mean "team". This finding bolsters the classification of Tapp & Clowes (2002) about "football" and "club" fans; idea that has been previously prematurely criticized by me.

According to Sullivan & Adcock (2002), in order for a customer to become loyal to a specific business an emotional attachment must happen in addition to an economic benefit. The findings here shown seem not to support the affirmations above, as it can be evidenced in the interviewee's answers to question 4 lines 1-6 and 5 lines 22-27. The interviewee's level of loyalty seems to have origins not related to economic benefits and emotional attachment to the club, but it is influenced by factors such as self-psychological benefit and social elements, and these other factors seem to influence his emotional attachment to his team. This is quite clear when he quotes on question 4 line 6 that he is getting advantage of the club and question 5 lines 11-14 when he says: "Ah...loyalty is a...I don't feel I can be loyal to the club, I feel I'm being more loyal to myself, if that's an appropriate phrase...I get so much enjoyment and pleasure out of the football and it's a big release from both family life, social upbringing and work stress point of view, I almost feel I've earned the right to go and therefore it's something I need as part of my routine." McGoldrick & Andre (1997) cited by Sullivan & Adcock (2002) affirm that elements such as affection, fidelity or commitment are inextricably linked to the concept of loyalty; therefore, in order to develop loyal behaviour, it is essential that a person be emotionally involved in a relationship. Independently on what triggers the interviewee's feelings of affection, fidelity or commitment, it can be said that the affirmation of McGoldrick & Andre (1997) finds here support.

The following interview's excerpts are related to assumption 2: the loyalty of devoted football fans to their teams starts from childhood because of family / peer influences.

Q7 excerpt lines 1-3; 4-9; 15-25; 26-29; 30; 31-34; 37-43.

"This, this is quite easy really. I was never as a child interested in football, because it wasn't a sport that my father followed. My father follows Wigan Rugby league football club, so occasionally he'd taken us on to watch the rugby and I really, really enjoyed that."

"...My older brother Chris was interested in football and did like Manchester United, but he hadn't been...We had a deputy head at school - I think his name was Mr. Clarkson - and he was from Sunderland and

Manchester United played Sunderland one Wednesday evening and he took the school minibus and he asked 12 lads if they wanted to go and some of the other lads, some friends of school came and ask me would I like to go? And I said yes, that sounds really…"

"…I went to the match on Wednesday night and absolutely enjoyed it; I realized what I've missing all my life and thought this is it, this is fantastic…atmosphere…it was a night match, it was dark, and the floodlights around was amazing, there was noise and a big crowd, a special huge city experience that I never experienced before. It involved travelling which I found exciting, which I'd never done before, we didn't't even have a car in the family, so it was a big…it was almost like a holiday, it was fantastic. And then one of the other guys at school got me a ticket for the derby match on the Saturday against Manchester City and again I went by a public transport, two sets of public transport to get there, set off very early in the morning to get there for an afternoon match…and again I had an absolute fabulous day, and then, that was it, I was hooked and never looked back."

"[Could we say that the first person who introduced you to football was this teacher in school?] Yes, he gave me the opportunity to go to a first division… to go to a football match at a football stadium, something that I'd never experienced before…So I'm eternally grateful to that gentleman."

"[So that was the moment when you decided to support Man United?] Yes."

"[And why not Sunderland?] Eh… why not Sunderland? Well, Sunderland obviously would be much further away and I think I was obviously slightly influenced by my brother that is a supporter of Manchester United and also quite a few friends of school were also supporters of Manchester United, so I think that had some influence…"

"[But do you think that your brother's and friends' influence was important for you to keep supporting Manchester United or even to decide to support Manchester United?]

I think it was probably informed in the decision, because the location that we live in Leyland it is the same distance to Liverpool as it is to Manchester and they were the sort of big teams around that area and Liverpool was very, very successful, so it would've been equally as a...you know...challenging to go to either Liverpool or Manchester, but I think the influence of the older brother Chris has probably really influenced me..."

The second assumption finds support from the comments of the interviewee about how he decided to support Man United. These findings also support the affirmation of Bristow & Sebastian (2001) who highlight that the high level of fans' loyalty towards a team can considerably be influenced by relatives/parents and surroundings throughout childhood.

The first affirmation that the loyalty of devoted football fans starts in their childhood is clearly bolstered on question 7 lines 4-9 and 15-25 related to the interviewee's first experience with a football match and on question 7 lines 26-29 when the participant shows his gratitude to his teacher who took him and his classmates to a football stadium for the first time. The affirmation about family or peer influences on the decision for the team to be supported is evidenced on question 7 lines 31-34 and 37-43 when the participant emphasizes the influence that his school mates had, but more importantly that his brother had on his decision to support Man United.

The following interview's excerpts are related to assumption 3: devoted football fans have an emotional attachment to their teams that is originated from regional/community/social status or pride reasons.

Q5 excerpt lines 6-8.

"When I did start to watch them, they were quite a mediocre team, even though they were famous club, the team itself was playing some pretty awful football, so I think…"

Q8 excerpt lines 1-2; 3-7; 13-16.

"No, I never lived in Manchester; always lived in Leyland which I think is about 27 miles away from Manchester."

"…the only way to professional teams in the area, again would be Preston North End or Wigan Athletic, therefore for me travelling 7 miles to Preston or 10 miles to Wigan…basically I never perceived them as a local team, as my team, and therefore when this opportunity arose I didn't see anything not wrong, but I didn't see any reason why shouldn't travel the extra distance to Manchester."

"…I think again Manchester because that was the opportunity given to me...somebody basically took me to Manchester and I think had somebody taken me to Preston I may well have been supporting Preston North End for the last 30 years."

Q9 excerpt lines 1-7.

"Well, yes. They now fall under the area sort of area of Greater Manchester, but the old boundaries they are definitely in Lancashire town and the Red Rose of Lancashire is sort of a...part of the club, and the club's crest they have red devil, they have a shipping company which is to do with the ship canal, they are originally called Luton Heath, probably 1880/90 they were first, first self conceived and there were a local railway team and then moved to Old Trafford and remained Manchester United. So I definitely see them as part of the, as part of Lancashire."

Q10 excerpt lines 1-6 and 8-12.

"No, I don't think there's any sort of status with it, I think certainly going back into the 70s it was very much a working class activity to go follow a football team and having left school I went to work in a local factory Leyland Motors as an electrician and tradition was that on the weekend a lot of workers would go follow their selected teams and the clubs then were absolutely full of working class people, certainly it was the norm to do that kind of activity, to support a team like that."

…"I think it's the financial aspect of supporting teams it's much more expensive these days and two, it's quite a social trendy thing to do, it's certainly opened up the sort of business side of it, the corporate side and hospitality side, it's been a huge growth industry and that really has only come down to the last sort of 15 years. Certainly, it was nonexistent when I started going."

Q11 excerpt lines 14-20.

"Had I not had a career and now I'd still, as we say, on the tools as a craftsman, then certainly during the period when we had two young children and my wife wasn't working, that probably would've made extremely difficult to finance the season ticket. Even though Julie and me had more challenging years, money was borrowed from…you know… by using a credit card to actually finance a season ticket and knew at that time that money was very tight within the family, but it was still seeing as far that I should have that social aspect for my working need."

Q12 excerpt lines 1-12 and 13-20.

"Definitely.

[Why ?]

Why am I proud?

I'm proud because of the loyalty high I've shown to the team. I'm proud of the fact that I've gone through good times and bad times. I find it a great way of communicating with people through football, through engaging in these relationships and as my role as manager at work, the fact that I can talk sensibly about football and I go to football it helps to move lots of barriers at work and therefore I have very good working relationships with people, with subordinates who work for me. And a lot of that is because they for some reason respect me more because I'm not just seen as a manager as a manager as the opposition, but I'm also seen as an ok guy because I socialize in similar when I'm going to the football etc."

"[So, the question was, if you're proud of being a Man United, and then I'd like to add another question, or are you proud of yourself for choosing Manchester United or supporting a team as a way of socializing with other people?]

I'm proud of supporting Manchester United, I'm proud of them because of the successes they have had and the style of the football they play and therefore because they play attractive attacking football, then I'm proud of that and I enjoy the sort of reward of that, the benefits of that. Yes, there's a certain self-pride in my loyalty to the club that I've been supporting for so many years…yeah, I've been telling lies if I did say that I wasn't."

Q14 excerpt lines 3-14.

"Because it is more than just enjoying the success. As you approach the game, if there's a game on Saturday, Thursday I start to think about it, Saturday morning I wake up excited like a child, I'll go out and buy a couple of newspapers and read about the game in anticipation, I'll be grinning from ear to ear at home, I'll be happy and shouting football songs, being a nuisance in general, I'll rush around getting all the jobs done and then I'll start to make flask and traditionally I always buy a big pack of mars bars for the people who sit around me, so I've got to make sure that everything's sorted, the car's got petrol in, etc. and, 12.30pm, I've early lunch 11.45, sandwich and then off we go 12.30. So it isn't just about the 90 min of football, but it's about feeling really good on the day of the match, and then we go to the match I meet my brother, which is fantastic, because I love my older brother, we have a real good chat, we put the worlds to right, we put the family to right and then we enjoy the football together and then we go off separate ways…"

Q18 excerpt lines 4-5.

"No, there's nothing that would entice me away. [Why?] Why is that? I don't know.

It is so embedded in me now and I couldn't change, not even with inducement stuff."

For the third assumption about the emotional attachment of a devoted football fan being based upon regional/community/social status or pride reasons, some interesting elements have been found.

McGoldrick and Andre (1997) cited by Sullivan & Adcock (2002) affirm that elements such as affection, fidelity or commitment are inextricably linked to the concept of loyalty; therefore, in order to develop loyal behaviour, it is essential that a person be emotionally involved in a relationship. This emotional involvement in turn is here believed to being originated from social and psychological elements, which finally will influence the attitude of football fans towards their teams. According to Gwinner & Swanson (2003), the degree of involvement of fans with a given team can vary and this variation will be influenced by the way a fan identifies themselves with such team. The question to be answered in hypothesis 3 is what factors determine this emotional involvement, consequently, attachment.

The case of regional or community reasons does not find much support from the information given by the participant. This is considerably clear through the fact that he lives in Leyland, which is about 27 miles away from Manchester (see question 8 lines 1-2). Moreover, by the time he chose to follow Man United F.C there were two other more local teams near Leyland such as Preston North End and Wigan Football Club, but nonetheless the interviewee chose a team which was not related to his birthplace (see question 8 lines 3-7). It seems that the choice of Man United was much more related to the opportunity to experience something new in life than to any reasons such as regional or community related attachment (see question 8 lines 13-16), despite the fact that the interviewee on question 9 lines 1-7 emphasizes that he sees Man United as being a representative of Lancashire.

The case of social status has not found support either, as the participant on question 10 lines 1-6 and 8-12 emphasizes the fact that when he started to follow football it was an activity for the working class rather than for the upper class as well as it was not a social trendy thing to do at the time. The previous idea is even more supported on question 5 lines 6-8. Also, he highlights on question 11 lines 14-20 the fact that following Man United's football is related to other social elements such as his work place and family.

The case of pride reasons finds support based on the information given on question 12 lines 1-12 and 13-20 when the interviewee pinpoints that he is proud of Man United for its achievements as a team, for its successes, which could be argued that it should be classified as social status reasons/feelings, but the author prefers a definition more related to the concept of Basking in Reflected Glory (BIRG) proposed by Cialdini et al (1976) cited by Mason (1999), which is influenced by the level of self-identity and emotional attachment to the team supported. The pride reasons here found seem to be related to some sort of self loyalty, to the character and beliefs of the interviewee as a person as well as his social life, (and this can be identified on question 5 lines 11-15 and question 12 lines 1-5 and 19-20), which seem to have a major influence on his emotional attachment to the team. Three basic elements can be allocated into the pride reasons classification for emotional attachment in this case: his determination to do anything well in life; his concept of loyalty as being an intrinsic feeling rather than influenced by external factors and his associations between his social life and football as being a balance regulator between the latter two (see excerpts of question 14 lines 3-14 and question 18 lines 4-5).

Despite the particular reasons of the interviewee's described above, the findings of this study seem to be in accordance with Sullivan & Adcock (2002), who emphasize that it is easier to retain a satisfied customer than attract a new one, however it does not always mean repeat purchases (see excerpts of questions 3 & 4). The findings of the present study also seem to support the following affirmation of Sheth et al (1999) cited by Bristow & Sebastian (2001) about the three fundamental components which contribute to consumer's brand loyalty: social and emotional identification, habit and long history with the brand (see excerpts of questions 5, 6, 12, 14 and 18).

The following interview's excerpts are related to assumption 4: tolerance and loyalty levels are reciprocally influential and determine the attitude of devoted football fans towards the teams supported by them.

Q5 excerpt lines 1; 3-8; 9-17; 18-28.

"I have a particular nature, when I decide to do something, I generally want to do it well…"

"…I started to follow my football team from 1975 and for me if you follow a team you follow a team, you don't one week when they play well follow them and the next when they're not playing so well, you're not interested. When I did start to watch them, they were quite a mediocre team, even though they were famous club, the team itself was playing some pretty awful football, so I think…"

"[Can you repeat the question? - Yes, the question is: what does it mean for you being loyal to someone, something? Something could be a cause or I don't know].

Ah...loyalty is a...I don't feel I can be loyal to the club, I feel I'm being more loyal to myself, if that's an appropriate phrase...I get so much enjoyment and pleasure out of the football and it's a big release from both family life, social upbringing and work stress point of view, I almost feel I've earned the right to go and therefore it's something I need as part of my routine. We're in the summer month now, July, and I'm already looking forward to the first game of the season, it just makes such a big difference. So, it's more out of passion and anticipation; which probably isn't based on logic at al."

"[Right, so you would consider your attitude towards your team, yeah, not as a loyal behaviour, yeah?] As loyalty, but as...that it would come from... the explanation would be for another reason, not really because you're loyal to the team, but because as you said for example, it is a way

for you to get rid of the stress of everyday life and so on, is that correct?
Yeah, I think that's correct. There's some loyalty with the team, as I don't
change teams, I have never changed teams, but the benefits are for
myself…being selfish…you know the enjoyment is purely for myself and
therefore that I think it's probably one of the main reasons why I still
continue to go and also think it helps from a family point of view that we
have our own interests, both husband and wife, we share a little bit of
interest in each other's hobbies etc., plus I give her some free time as well.
So, it has for me also other benefits."

Q6 excerpt lines 1-4; 5-6; 5-11.

"NO, I couldn't do that. I couldn't do that. Why not? Why not…because I
think you've got to take with the good times and the bad times, you gotta
take the rough with the smooth and there's no way I would move or
defect from one club to another. I don't know, my principles are… it
wouldn't allow me to do that."

"[So, wouldn't that be loyalty then?] Yes, I suppose it would be. It would be loyalty, yes, but I never thought of it that way..."

"...you know if I go back to the 80s we played some poor football, very poor football and the crowds were dropping significantly, from an average of 48.000 down to that of 35.000, but I would never consider not going, I'd still go, I'd get excited with the anticipation, I'd enjoy the match regardless of the result and no doubt mourn about it for the next two or three days, but I'd be back for the next game. So yes, there's a degree of loyalty."

Q12 excerpt lines 16-20.

"I'm proud of supporting Manchester United, I'm proud of them because of the successes they have had and the style of the football they play and therefore because they play attractive attacking football, then I'm proud of that and I enjoy the sort of reward of that, the benefits of that. Yes, there's a certain self-pride in my loyalty to the club that I've been supporting for so many years...yeah, I've been telling lies if I did say that I wasn't."

Q13 excerpt lines 1-4 and 5-11.

"Yes, they've already done, under performed and my expectations are that they will not perform as well as they have done...in the future and how soon in the future I don't know, but I fully expect. I've often thought that as the club starts to underperform, I have visions of myself sat in a half empty stand. But, yeah, my vision is that I'll still be going."

"[You think that if you were not loyal as you are now, do you think that performance would be an element to motivate you to decide not to support anymore that team?]

It's a difficult question to answer, but I know a lot of people, I know there are fans already I sit with, who would pick and choose the games because we're not playing as well and only when we start to play well they'll start to come to the games, so loyalty is often based on performance, but for myself, I hope it wouldn't be based pure on performance."

Q14 excerpt lines 1-3.

"Yeah, definitely.

[Why?]

Because it is more than just enjoying the success..."

Q18 excerpt lines 1-5.

"No, definitely not.

[Say, they offered you to get to know their players, or they would give you a car or free season tickets...]

No, there's nothing that would entice me away. [Why?] Why is that? I don't know.

It is so embedded in me now and I couldn't change, not even with inducement stuff."

The 4th assumption supports the idea that loyalty and tolerance levels are reciprocally influential and determines the attitude of devoted football fans towards their teams. This assumption finds support from the fact that undoubtedly the level of loyalty and tolerance of the interviewee is high, as it can be shown through his comments on excerpts of questions 5, 6, 12, 13, 14 and 18 (see above). Therefore, it is plausible to affirm that loyalty and tolerance have an influence on each other and may determine the attitude of devoted football fans towards their teams. However, another element needs to considered in this particular case, as the interviewee considers following Man United's football as a way of having a relief from family and work place stresses (see questions 5 lines 12-14, 11 lines 19-20, 12 lines 5-12, 14 lines 18-21, 16 lines 4-11, 17 lines 1-6). In addition, his character as a person probably explains his loyalty and tolerance levels. His need for a palliative solution for his stressful work and family life is well emphasized by his wording and football in his case seems to keep the balance in his life - because of the importance that football has on his personal life as a social and psychological regulator, the interviewee's emotional attachment to the his team seems to be increased by this factor. The previous idea interestingly complements or better said, adds to the 3rd assumption as another element that may influence the emotional attachment of devoted football fans, which is the socialization and psychological relief from everyday life.

The concept of zone of tolerance is not new within management literature (Lovelock & Wright, 2002; Groenroos, 2000) and it is related to the level of tolerance a consumer holds towards a service provider. This will directly be determined by the consumers' conception of quality and emotional attachment to the service provider. Although the present work does not offer a valid instrument to assess the relationship between that level of tolerance and loyalty and their mutual influence, the results found from the interviewee's affirmations tend to support the 4th assumption somewhat. In addition to what has been said above, emotional attachment is a fundamental element for the existence of loyalty feelings (Sullivan & Adcock, 2002), no matter the reasons for such emotional attachment. Therefore, it is plausible to affirm that tolerance and loyalty levels are indeed mutually influential; however, a deeper analysis on this subject through other researches is necessary before any assumptions can be made with accuracy.

The following interview's excerpts are related to assumption 5: the consumerist and materialistic mentality of postmodernist society have not influenced the loyalty of devoted football fans.

Q3 excerpt lines 1-4.

"I'm a consumer or a customer because I purchase the season ticket every year and purchase the programmes. Yes, but I also won't be misguided, I also think I can see the minimum that I have to do to get the maximum out of the football team, cause it's the team, it's the football that I love, that I enjoy."

Q4 excerpt lines 1-6.

"Eh…both parties benefiting from it…I haven't really thought of it that way, before…yes, I suppose I'm purchasing a form of entertainment, and obviously I feel that it's value for money otherwise I wouldn't be going. But I know that I benefit from the point of view that I enjoy watching a football team; that football team has developed significantly over the later years and has been very successful and I've been fortunate enough to get to enjoy those in my years of life time their successes. So, yes I'm getting advantage of the club."

Q5 excerpt lines 22-25.

"There's some loyalty with the team, as I don't change teams, I have never

changed teams, but the benefits are for myself...being selfish...you know

the enjoyment is purely for myself and therefore that I think it's probably

one of the main reasons why I still continue to go..."

Q6 excerpt lines 1-4.

"NO, I couldn't do that. I couldn't do that. Why not? Why not...because I

think you've got to take with the good times and the bad times, you gotta

take the rough with the smooth and there's no way I would move or

defect from one club to another. I don't know, my principles are... it

wouldn't allow me to do that."

Q13 excerpt lines 1-4.

"Yes. They've already done, under performed and my expectations are

that they will not perform as well as they have done...in the future and how soon in the future I don't know, but I fully expect, I've often thought that as the club start to underperform I have visions of myself sat in a half empty stand. But, yeah, my vision is that I'll still be going."

Q14 excerpt lines 1-14.

"Yeah, definitely.

[Why?]

Because it is more than just enjoying the success. As you approach the game, if there's a game on Saturday, Thursday I start to think about it, Saturday morning I wake up excited like a child, I'll go out and buy a couple of newspapers and read about the game in anticipation, I'll be grinning from ear to ear at home, I'll be happy and shouting football songs, being a nuisance in general, I'll rush around getting all the jobs done and then I'll start to make flask and traditionally I always buy a big pack of mars bars for the people who sit around me, so I've got to make sure that everything's sorted, the car's got petrol in, etc. and, 12.30pm, I've early lunch 11.45, sandwich and then off we go 12.30. So it isn't just about the 90 min of football, but it's about feeling really good on the day of the match, and then we go to the match I meet my brother, which is fantastic, because I love my older brother, we have a real good chat, we put the worlds to right, we put the family to right and then we enjoy the football together…"

Q18 excerpt lines 1-5.

"No, definitely not.

[Say, they offered you to get to know their players, or they would give you a car or free season tickets…]

No, there's nothing that would entice me away. [Why?] Why is that? I don't know.

It is so embedded in me now and I couldn't change, not even with inducement stuff."

Smart (1993) highlights that there is a relationship between postmodernism and what he calls 'the erosion of cultural hierarchies', the concern about new technologies and the spread of consumerism. Morrison et al (1999) points out the concept of post-modernist consumer challenge which is related to the transition in customer's traits from straightforward to extremely heterogeneous, open to the new and behaviourally volatile. Cova & Sevenfold (1993) cited by Morrison et al (1999) affirm that post-modernist individuals are free to choose what is most suitable to suffice their whims, which leads to what they call a *'general promiscuity and playful mixing of codes'*. They also affirm that it may well be possible that a post-modernist consumer assumes similar behavioural patterns. However, the findings of the present study do not support such affirmations as it can be shown below.

The 5th assumption finds support in the comments of the interviewee in the answers to questions 6, 13, 14 and 18 (see above). Although he tends to highlight on questions 3 lines 1-4, 4 lines 1-6, 5 lines 22-25 and 14 lines

1-14 the individual benefits that he gets from following Man United, these again seem to be related to his social life, to some extent a need and not a whim that can be sufficed by purchasing or accepting some sort of financial benefit or status "bribery". This can be understood if we simply imaginatively remove from his life the opportunity to enjoy the football matches, as a consequence, it would have a negative impact on his family and working life. In addition, there is no sign of possible persuasive offer that would induce him to change teams or switch his loyalty to another club, as it can be pointed out on questions 6 lines 1-4, 13 lines 1-4 and 18 lines 1-5. This leads to the belief that there exist personal values such as loyalty that may not be passive of the corruptive influence of the post-modern mentality of today's society, no matter the motives for holding such personal values as fundamental in people's life, more specifically in the case of the subject here studied.

Conclusion

Much has been emphasized within management literature about the importance of building strategies to bolster customers' retention and loyalty through a continuing relationship among suppliers and customers in order to create an advantage for both parties. Also, that each contact with the customers can be an opportunity to develop relationships (Gumesson, 2002; Sullivan and Adcock, 2002; Stone, Woodock and Machtynger, 2000; Lumsdon, 1997). Recently this new marketing concept has been applied in sports marketing realm, as pinpointed by Kelley et al (1999) - this trend seems to have its basis on the fact that traditional marketing approaches do not suffice to address issues related to football fans attitude and behaviour. Supporting the previous affirmation, Mullin et al. (2000) offer a cluster of statements from different perspectives with the intention to point out why sports fans are unique; some of them are mentioned next: Firstly, they say that sports fans are highly involved with the sports product because of their personal identification with a given sport; then, as sports are publicly consumed, customer satisfaction is related to social facilitation; the sport product is inconsistent and unpredictable; finally, sport is quasi demographically universal. These ideas have underpinned the current research initiative, as the author believes that devoted football fans can by no means be compared to ordinary consumers because of their high level of emotional attachment and loyalty to their teams (Tapp & Clowes, 2002).

There exist findings from researches that point to the belief that an inside-fans-domain approach may be suitable to understand better fans' attitude and behaviour, and consequently to develop ways to motivate fans to engage more actively in supporting activities towards their teams (Gwinner & Swanson, 2003; Hunt, Bristol & Bashaw, 1999), and it is based on this idea that a different marketing concept named as 'Tribal Marketing' has emerged within literature. Cova & Cova (2002) highlight that a tribe is defined as a network of heterogeneous people who are related by a shared emotion or passion; that these same people can act collectively for a specific motive and therefore they cannot be seen an ordinary consumer, but as advocates. Moreover, the authors affirm that rituals are the form tribes have to express their shared beliefs and social belonging and that examples of these rituals can include specific clothing, magical or ritual words, idols, icons, etc - such a definition could not draw a better picture of loyal football fans. It has been inspired by this concept and based on social identity theories that this research came to exist, as devoted football fans do show many 'tribal' characteristics and therefore should be approached by marketers in a way different from that used for ordinary consumers.

This academic work aimed at reaching this inside-fans-domain approach through the use of a qualitative research approach and using the perspective of a devoted fan (Hunt et al, 1999) to deeply understand the real reasons why devoted fans are highly loyal to their teams, why they become and remain loyal even if the team supported goes through a hardship moment, and how they conceive their relationship with their supported clubs. By finding out such motives, it would become possible to understand why the zone of tolerance of devoted football fans is high and what sort of relation there exists between loyalty and tolerance levels. In addition, from such findings it was here believed to be possible to improve or even develop marketing strategies to exploit such elements related to devoted football fans' justifications for their loyalty in order to encourage them to become even more loyal to their teams and, possibly, to encourage them to engage in a word of mouth process to convince other less loyal fans of the benefits of becoming a devoted fan. Moreover, such findings would help marketers to promote the emergence of new-devoted fans.

The findings of this research seem to be promising, although it is far from presuming that it can generally be applied. They are nonetheless indicators that different marketing strategies may be more effective if a deep holistic understanding of football fans takes place. Based on the findings here presented it is possible to conclude that the zone of tolerance of devoted fans are high because of their high loyalty to their teams, but also that their level of loyalty can be influenced by the natural level of tolerance of an individual. This tolerance level seems to be determined by an individual's personality and beliefs and, therefore, by his experiences with their families throughout their growing-up process. It is also possible to affirm that the level of loyalty of a devoted fan may reach a steady-state depending on the personality and beliefs of such fans, which, in turn leads to the belief that within the universe of devoted fans levels of loyalty can vary and may be explained by many different reasons - in the case of the subject here studied, his family and work experiences' balance seem to be regulated by his adherence to Man United F.C as a loyal supporter, as well as his personal beliefs are strengthened by his attitude towards the club. Therefore, on this specific case, it does seem to be a complex task to find ways of instigating loyal fans to engage in word of mouth or to become part-time marketers (Gummesson, 2002) for reasons each individual has to become a devoted fan which may not be commonly shared amongst the same type of fans.

However, it seems that emphasizing the value of the social experience and facilitating it to happen (Mullin et al, 2000), may help loyal fans to be even more satisfied with their teams and, it is never enough to pinpoint that satisfaction is a premise for engagement in word of mouth behaviour.

The participant's explanations about how he has become a supporter of Man United F.C. indicate that a loyal behaviour starts during childhood influenced by persons who have an important meaning for the child such as siblings or mates of their age. In addition, it is not only by choosing a team when the first opportunity for that is given during childhood in itself that determines their future attitude towards the team supported, but also the whole new social interaction and positive experience associated with football at that moment of that very choice - this consequently seems to trigger the beginning of an emotional attachment to the team chosen. In the case of the subject here studied, there are indications that his emotional attachment has been strengthened throughout the last 46 years by the fact that he can still re-experience that first time when he went to a football match (see question 15 lines 1-11). Furthermore, following a football team has become so intensively part of his life that it serves now as a balance regulator for his family and work life (see question 16 lines 1-11). Therefore, it is possible to affirm that in order to develop a loyal attitude towards a brand (in this case, football teams) a person needs to have a first positive experience associated with the brand and, most interestingly, the experience itself may be influenced by factors such as social interaction, discovering of a new world and by the fact that it is simply the first time that an individual feels a positive emotional impact never before experienced, rather than self-identification with a team. Conclusively, sports marketers should concentrate their efforts on to offer children these sorts of experiences that should not necessarily be associated with commercial purposes or directly associated with the exploitation of team's name; an approach in the present for the future.

Finally, it has been found that the loyalty of the subject studied seems not to be passive of the influence of the materialistic and consumerist mentality of postmodernist society. There are indications that his level of loyalty is much related to his personality and beliefs, and that these elements are strong enough to overcome the influence of postmodernism. However, the findings leave space for further investigations to find out, for instance, whether his loyalty as an intrinsically motivated value and independent on external reinforcements is what keeps him loyal to Man United or whether the role of his team/football as a psychological balance regulator determines his level of loyalty (see questions 5 lines 11-15, 6 lines 1-4 and 18 lines 1-5).

The findings here shown are not exhaustive and do not even cover the entire world of football fans, the devoted fans. However, the results of this study have supported most of the assumptions pointed out previously and hopefully will serve as a motivator for new research initiatives in this field. Other aspects such as the relationship between zone of tolerance and loyalty levels as well as the origins and feeders of the emotional attachment towards a team can be more explored in order to understand what kind of relationship football fans have with their clubs/teams, and what function a football team has in football fans' life. Inasmuch as what has been said, it seems that typifying or classifying football fans based on observations about their behaviour from an outside perspective is far from being the best way for marketers to understand how to approach and target this unique type of 'consumers'.

Bibliography

Ashforth, B.E. & Mael, F. (1989), **Social identity theory and the organization**, *Academy of Management Review*, Vol.14 No.1 pp. 20-30.

Ben-Porat, A. (2000), **Overseas sweetheart**, *Journal of Sport & Social Issues*, Vol.24 No.4 pp. 344-350.

Berg, B.L. (2001), **Qualitative Research Methods For The Social Sciences**, (4th Ed.), London, Allyn and Bacon.

Bristow, D.N. & Sebastian, R.J. (2001), **Holy Cow! Wait 'til next year! A closer look at the brand loyalty of Chicago Cubs baseball fans**, *Journal of Consumer Marketing*, Vol.18 No.3 pp. 256-275.

Christopher, M., Payne, A. & Ballantyne, D. (2002), **Relationship Marketing**, Butter-Heinemann, Oxford.

Cialdini, R.B., Borden, R.J., Thorne, A., Walker, M.R., Freeman, S. & Sloan, L.R. (1976), **Basking in reflected glory: three (football) field studies**, *Journal of Personality and Social Psychology*, Vol.34 pp. 366-377.

Connor, S. (2001), **Postmodernist Culture: an introduction to theories of the contemporary**, (2nd Ed.), Oxford, Blackwell.

Cova, B. & Cova V. (2002), **Tribal marketing: The tribalisation of society and its impact on the conduct of marketing**, *European Journal of Marketing*, Vol.36, No.5/6 pp.595-620.

Davidoff, D.M. (1994), **Contact: Customer Service and the Hospitality and Tourism Industry**, London, Practice Hall.

Ferrand, A. & Pages, M. (1999), **Image management in sport organisations: the creation of value**, *European Journal of Marketing*, Vol. 33 No3/4, pp. 387-401.

Gabbott, M & Hogg, G. (1997), **Contemporary Services Marketing Management**, London, The Dryden Press.

Glyn, W.J. & Barnes, J.G. (1995), **Understanding Services Management**, Chichester, Wiley.

Groenroos, C. (2000), **Service Management and Marketing**, (2nd Ed.), Chichester, Wiley.

Gummesson, E. (2002), **Total Relationship Marketing Management: From 4Ps to 30Rs**, Oxford, Butterworth-Heinemann.

Gwinner, K & Swanson, S.R. (2003), **A model of fan identification:**

antecedents and sponsorship outcomes**, *Journal of Services Marketing*, Vol.17 No.3 pp. 275-294.

Harbord, D. & Szymanski, S. (2004), **Football Trials**, *European Competition Law Review*, pp. 1-6.

Hendrich, C. (1977), **Perspectives on Social Psychology**, London, LEA.

Hoffman, K.G. & Bateson, J.E.G (2002), **Essential of Services Marketing: Concepts, Strategies & Cases**, (2nd Ed.), Orlando, Harcourt College Publications.

Hogg, M.A. & Turner, J.C. (1985), **Interpersonal attraction, social identification and psychological group formation**, *European Journal of Social Psychology*, Vol.15 pp. 51-66.

Hunt, K.A., Bristol, T. & Bashaw, R.E. (1999), **A conceptual approach to classifying sports fans**, *Journal of Services Marketing*, Vol.13 No.6 pp. 439-452.

Jameson, F. (1995), **Postmodernism or, the cultural logic of late capitalism**, (3rd Ed.), London, Verso.

Kelley, S.W., Hoffman, K.D. & Carter, S. (1999), **Franchise relocation and sport introduction: a sports marketing case study of the **Carolina Hurricanes' fan adoption plan**, *Journal of Services Marketing*, Vol.13 No.6 pp. 469-480.

Kiesler, C. A., Collins, B. E. and Miller, N. (1969), **Attitude Change: a critical analysis of theoretical approaches**, London, John Wiley & Sons.

Lovelock, C. H. and Wright, L. (2002), **Principles of Service Marketing and Management**, (2nd Ed.), New Jersey, Prentice Hall.

Lovelock, C.H. (1992), **Managing Services: Marketing, Operations and Human Resources**, (2nd Ed.), London, Practice Hall.

Lumsdon, L. (1997), **Tourism Marketing**, London, Thomson Learning.

Mason, D.S. (1999), **What is the sports product and who buys it? The Marketing of professional sports leagues**, *European Journal of Marketing*, Vol.33 No. 3/4 pp. 402-418.

Merton, R. (1949), **Social theory and social structure**, Glencoe, Free Press.

Middleton, V.T.C. and Clarke, J. (2001), **Marketing in Travel and Tourism**, (3rd Ed.), Oxford, Butterworth-Heinemann.

Morrison, A., Rimmington, M. & Williams, C. (1999), **Entrepreneurship in the Hospitality, Tourism & Leisure Industries**, Oxford,

Butterworth-Heinemann.

Mullin, B., Hardy, S. & Sutton, W. (2000), **Sport Marketing**, (2nd Ed.), Leeds, Human Kinetics.

Normann, R. (2000), **Service Management**, (3rd Ed.), Wiley, Chichester.

Padgett, D.K. (1998), **Qualitative Methods in Social Work: challenges and rewards**, London, SAGE.

Palmer, A. (1998), **Principles of Services Marketing**, (2nd Ed.), London, McGraw Hill.

Schaaf, P. (1995), **Sports Marketing: it's not just a game anymore**, New York: Prometheus Books.

Shannon, J.R. (1999), **Sports marketing: an examination of academic marketing publication**, *Journal of Services Marketing*, Vol.13 No.6 pp.517-534.

Schmenner, R.W. (1986), **How Can Service Businesses Survive and Prosper?,** *Sloan Management Review Association*, pp.31-41.

Shostack, G. L. (1987), **Service Positioning Through Structural Change**, *Journal of Marketing*, Vol. 51 pp. 34-43.

Schwarz, C., Klein, V., Davidson, G., Graham, J., Martin, M. A. R., McDonald, F., McGauran, F., Seaton, A. & Sergeant, H. (1991), **Chambers Concise Dictionary**, Edinburgh, Chambers.

Smart, B. (1993), **Postmodernity**, London, Routledge.

Sullivan, M. & Adcock, D. (2002), **Retail Marketing**, London, Thomson.

Tajfel, H. (1978), **Differentiation Between Social Groups: Studies in the Social Psychology of Intergroup Relations**, London, Academic Press.

Tapp, A. & Clowes, J. (2002), **From "carefree casuals" to "professional wonderers": segmentation possibilities for football supporters**, *European Journal of Marketing*, Vol.36 No.11/12 pp.1248-1269.

Theodorakis, N., Kambitsis, C., Laios, A. & Koustelios, A. (2001), **Relationship between measures of service quality and satisfaction of spectators in professional sports**, *Managing Service Quality*, Vol.11 No.6 pp. 431-438.

Thomas, R. (1998), **The Management of Small Tourism and Hospitality Firms**, London, Cassel.